VIOLA ▼ BOOK THREE

ESSENTIAL TECHNIQUE
FOR STRINGS

A COMPREHENSIVE STRING METHOD

MICHAEL ALLEN • ROBERT GILLESPIE • PAMELA TELLEJOHN HAYES

INTERMEDIATE TECHNIQUE STUDIES

THREE MAJOR SECTIONS
I. **Higher Positions and Shifting**
II. **Keys and Scales**
III. **Bowings, Rhythms and Vibrato**

T0055358

Essential Technique for Strings is a book of studies to help the intermediate player develop the skills necessary for playing in an orchestra. Chronologically, it follows Book 2 of *Essential Elements for Strings;* however, it is designed as a multi-use technique book for use within a string orchestra setting. The various sections of the book are organized so that you may use them in the way that best suits your individual needs.

As you progress with your musical training you will become involved in a variety of performances. Always observe proper concert etiquette by being well prepared, dressing appropriately, being on time, and remembering all equipment. Show respect when others are playing by listening attentively and applauding at the appropriate time.

As your musical experiences continue, you will enjoy discussing various opportunities that are available to musicians. Careers include teaching, performing, conducting, and composing. No matter what profession you choose, there are always opportunities available to you to continue your musical involvement. You can continue to play your instrument in community, civic, or church orchestras. One can also attend concerts and become a supporter of the arts. Whether you choose music as a vocation or avocation, we hope it will always be an important part of your life. We wish you the very best for a lifetime of musical success.

To create an account, visit:
www.essentialelementsinteractive.com

Student Activation Code
"E3VA-2706-6920-9467"

ISBN 978-0-634-06930-7

Copyright © 2004 by HAL LEONARD CORPORATION
International Copyright Secured   All Rights Reserved

HAL•LEONARD®
CORPORATION
7777 W. BLUEMOUND RD. P.O. BOX 13819 MILWAUKEE, WI 53213

THIRD POSITION ON THE D STRING

1. TUNING TRACK

2.

3.

4.

THIRD POSITION ON THE A STRING

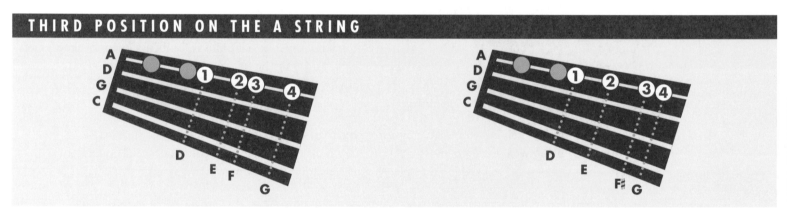

5.

6.

7.

8.

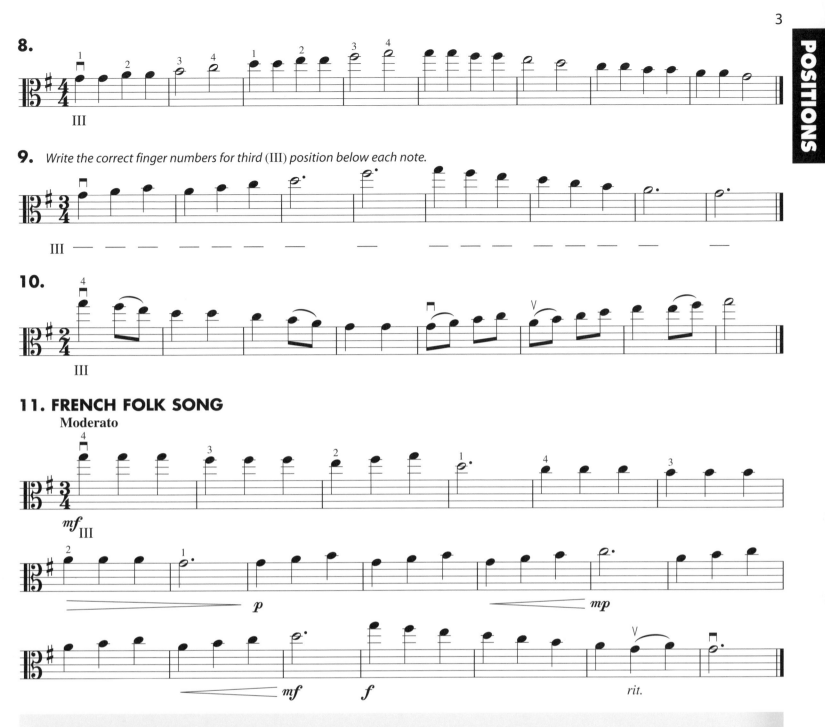

9. *Write the correct finger numbers for third (III) position below each note.*

10.

11. FRENCH FOLK SONG

Moderato

The **symphony** has its roots in late 18th century central Europe. Haydn, a German composer, wrote more than one hundred symphonies and is credited with setting a standard of symphonic composition that was a model for those who followed. Haydn's contemporary, Mozart, added to the symphony by expanding melodic content as well as form. Beethoven brought the symphony into the Romantic age by further expanding form as well as changing instrumentation. Following Beethoven were numerous Romantic composers such as Tchaikovsky, Brahms, and Dvořák who developed harmony, rhythm, and folk elements.

By the late 1800s, Mahler's and Bruckner's compositions were so developed that they hardly resembled the symphonies of Haydn. Listen to recordings of symphonies from various style periods and attend live performances whenever possible. Describe the various sounds and instruments that you hear.

12. SYMPHONY NO. 1 THEME

Allegro

Gustav Mahler (1860–1911)

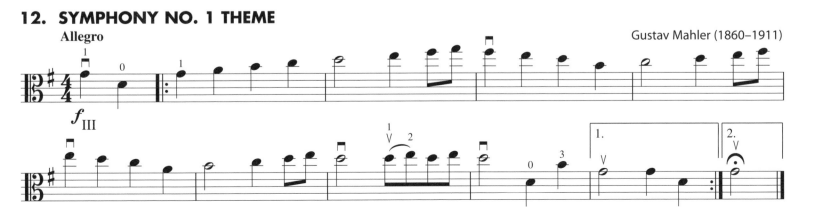

4

Natural Harmonic
(Review)

Natural harmonics are tones created by a vibrating string divided into equal sections. To play an octave higher than an open string, lightly touch the string exactly half way between the bridge and the nut. In the following examples, harmonics are indicated by a "○" above a note, plus a fingering number. $\overset{4}{\circ}$ indicates a harmonic played with the fourth finger.

13.

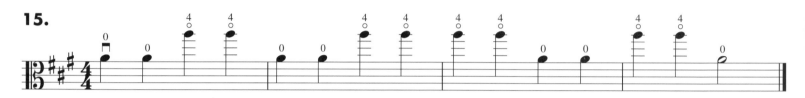

14.

15.

16.

Shifting
(Review)

Slide your left hand smoothly and lightly to a new location on the fingerboard, indicated by a dash (–). Be sure your thumb moves with your hand.

17.

18.

19.

20.

SHIFTING ON THE D AND A STRINGS

21.

22.

23.

24.

25.

26.

27.

28.

6

Violas sometimes read notation in treble clef which is indicated by the following sign: 𝄞.
The folllowing pitches are played in the same place on your instrument:

29.

30.

31.

32.

33.

34.

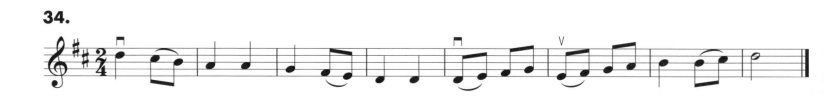

35. CAN CAN

Jacques Offenbach (1819–1880)

Presto ◁ *Very fast*

D.S. al Fine

Play until you see the **D.S. al Fine**. Then go back to the sign (𝄋) and play until the word **Fine**. D.S. is the abbreviation for **Dal Segno**, or "from the sign," and **Fine** means "the end."

---

36. MARCH IN D

Johann Sebastian Bach (1685–1750)

Marziale ◁ *March-like style*

SHIFTING ON THE E STRING *(violin)*

37.

38.

39.

40.

SHIFTING ON THE D STRING

41.

42.

43.

44.

45.

46.

47.

48.

SHIFTING ON THE A STRING

THIRD POSITION ON THE G STRING

Remember to adjust the placement, weight, and speed of the bow to produce the best tone quality on the G string.

57.

58.

59.

60.

61.

62.

Rallentando   *rall.* – Gradually slower (same as *ritardando*).

63. LONG LONG AGO

64. BLUE BELLS OF SCOTLAND

SHIFTING ON THE G STRING

65.

66.

67.

68.

12

POSITIONS

SECOND POSITION ON THE D STRING

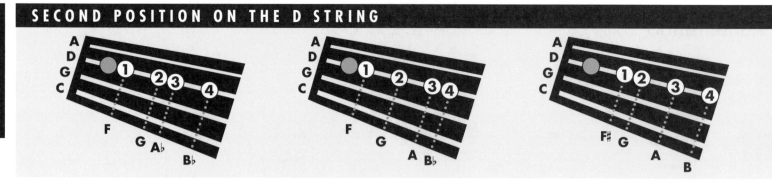

69.

70.

71.

72.

SECOND POSITION ON THE A STRING

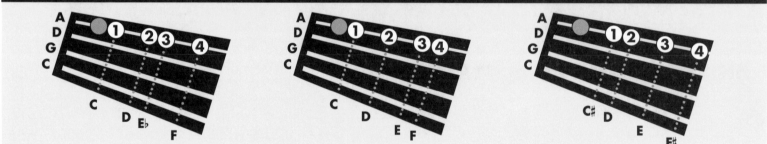

73.

74.

75.

76.

77.

78.

79.

Dynamics

pp – *pianissimo* (play very softly) ff – *fortissimo* (play very loudly)
Remember to use proper bow placement, weight, and speed to produce the best possible tone.

80. ROW, ROW, ROW YOUR BOAT – Round

Moderato   Traditional

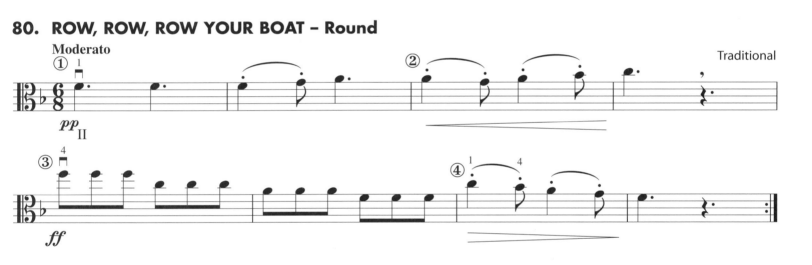

A **Concerto** is a composition in several movements for solo instrument and orchestra. Exercise 81 is the theme from the first movement of the *Concerto for Violin and Orchestra* by **Ludwig van Beethoven**, composed while author William Wordsworth was writing his poem *I Wandered Lonely as a Cloud*. A special feature of the concerto is the cadenza, which was improvised, or made up, by the soloist during a concert. Improvising and creating your own music is great fun. Try it if you have not already.

81. THEME FROM VIOLIN CONCERTO

Andante   Ludwig van Beethoven (1770–1827)

on the G string

14

THIRD POSITION ON THE C STRING

POSITIONS

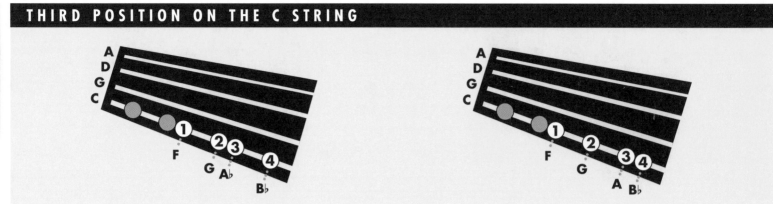

82.

83.

84.

85.

86.

87.

88. OH! SUSANNAH

Allegretto

Stephen C. Foster (1826–1864)

Music can be created and arranged by changing rhythms and notes of an existing example. Create your own arrangement of *Oh! Susannah* by changing the rhythms and melodic phrases. Perform your arrangement for others.

Example 1: Changing rhythms

Example 2: Changing melodic phrases

89. FIELD SONG

Moderato

Southern American Folk Song

SHIFTING ON THE C STRING

90.

91.

92.

93.

POSITIONS

SECOND POSITION ON THE E STRING (violin)

94.

II

95.

II

96. *Watch the clef sign!*

III

97.

III

98.

III

99.

III

FOR VIOLAS ONLY

Write the note names underneath each note. Notice the clef signs.

100. JOLLY GOOD FELLOW

Copy exercise 100 on a piece of manuscript paper. Be sure to include the time signature, dynamics, and bowings.

101. MAY TIME

W. A. Mozart (1756–1791)

SHIFTING ON THE A AND D STRINGS

102.

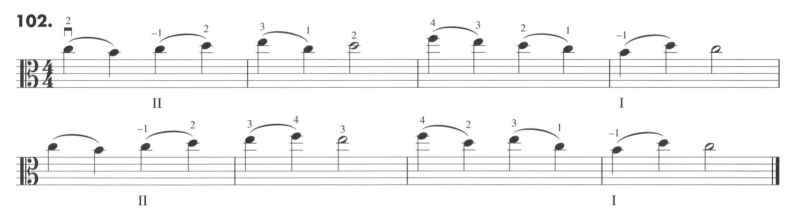

103.

C MAJOR

MAJOR KEYS

FINGER PATTERNS

Each finger pattern is a combination of whole steps and half steps. In the open hand pattern in third position, there is a whole step between each finger. Other patterns have half steps between fingers 1–2, 2–3 or 3–4.

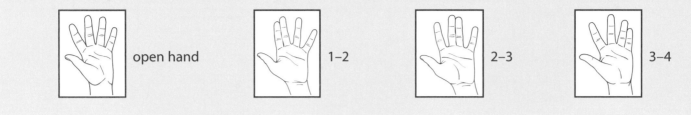

open hand   1–2   2–3   3–4

104. FINGER PATTERNS IN C MAJOR – First Position

(violin, bass)

105. FINGER PATTERNS IN C MAJOR – Third Position

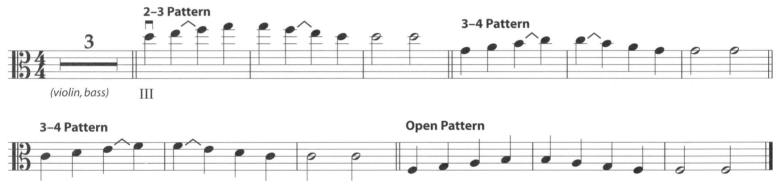

(violin, bass)   III

Identify two important elements of performing scales and arpeggios accurately. As you play each of these in the various keys presented in this section, check to make sure you are able to do these things.

106. C MAJOR SCALE

107. C MAJOR ARPEGGIO

108. THIRDS IN C MAJOR

109. THE BRITISH GRENADIERS

English

Johann Sebastian Bach is probably best remembered as an organist and church musician, but he also wrote hundreds of compositions for the royal courts of Germany and Austria. For example, *The Brandenburg Concertos* are works for instrumental ensembles dedicated to the court at Brandenburg. Bach lived at the same time the original thirteen colonies were being settled by European immigrants. The chorales in this book can be performed by the entire orchestra, or a small ensemble. Following any performance, always evaluate your playing and make a list of things to improve.

HISTORY

110. CHORALE IN C   A = Melody. B = Harmony.   J. S. Bach (1685–1750)

MAJOR KEYS

G MAJOR

MAJOR KEYS

FINGER PATTERNS

Each finger pattern is a combination of whole steps and half steps. In the open hand pattern in third position, there is a whole step between each finger. Other patterns have half steps between fingers 1–2, 2–3 or 3–4.

111. FINGER PATTERNS IN G MAJOR – First Position

(violin, bass)

112. FINGER PATTERNS IN G MAJOR – Third Position

(violin, bass) III

113. G MAJOR SCALE

114. G MAJOR ARPEGGIO   *Identify the intervals before playing.*

115. THIRDS IN G MAJOR

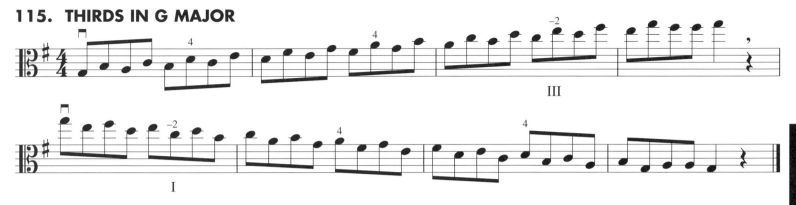

116. DONA NOBIS PACEM – Canon/Round

Traditional Canon

117. CHORALE IN G   **A** = Melody. **B** = Harmony.

J. S. Bach (1685–1750)

MAJOR KEYS

D MAJOR

FINGER PATTERNS

Each finger pattern is a combination of whole steps and half steps. In the open hand pattern in third position, there is a whole step between each finger. Other patterns have half steps between fingers 1–2, 2–3 or 3–4.

open hand   1–2   2–3   3–4

118. FINGER PATTERNS IN D MAJOR – First Position

(violin, bass)

119. FINGER PATTERNS IN D MAJOR – Third Position

(violin, bass)   III

120. D MAJOR SCALE

121. D MAJOR ARPEGGIO

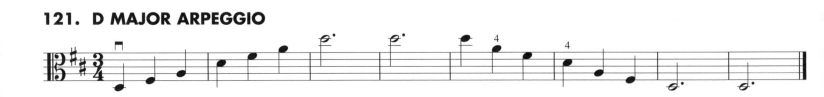

122. THIRDS IN D MAJOR

123. TRUMPET VOLUNTARY Jeremiah Clarke (1674–1707)

124. CHORALE IN D **A** = Melody. **B** = Harmony. J. S. Bach (1685–1750)

A MAJOR

MAJOR KEYS

FINGER PATTERNS

Each finger pattern is a combination of whole steps and half steps. In the open hand pattern in first position, a half step occurs between the open string and first finger. In the open hand pattern in third position, there is a whole step between each finger. Other patterns have half steps between fingers 1–2, 2–3 or 3–4.

open hand   1–2   2–3   3–4

125. FINGER PATTERNS IN A MAJOR – First Position

(violin, bass)

126. FINGER PATTERNS IN A MAJOR – Third Position

(violin, bass)

127. A MAJOR SCALE   *Mark all the half steps before playing.*

△ *New position*

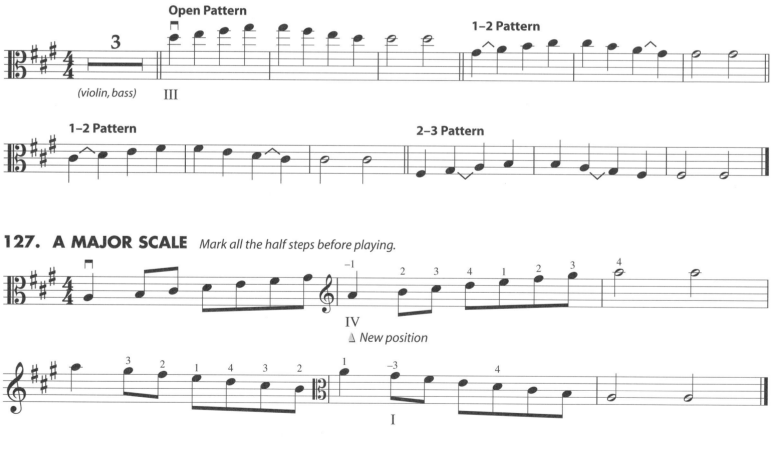

128. A MAJOR ARPEGGIO

129. THIRDS IN A MAJOR

130. THE YELLOW ROSE OF TEXAS

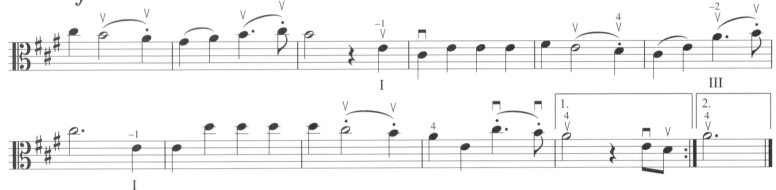

131. CHORALE IN A A = Melody. B = Harmony.

J. S. Bach (1685–1750)

MAJOR KEYS

F MAJOR

MAJOR KEYS

FINGER PATTERNS

Each finger pattern is a combination of whole steps and half steps. In the open hand pattern, a half step occurs between the open string and first finger. Other patterns have half steps between fingers 1–2, 2–3 or 3–4.

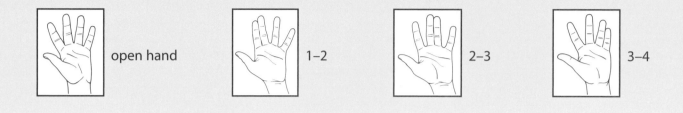

132. FINGER PATTERNS IN F MAJOR – First Position

(violin, bass)

133. FINGER PATTERNS IN F MAJOR – Third Position

(violin, bass)   III

134. F MAJOR SCALE

135. F MAJOR ARPEGGIO

136. THIRDS IN F MAJOR

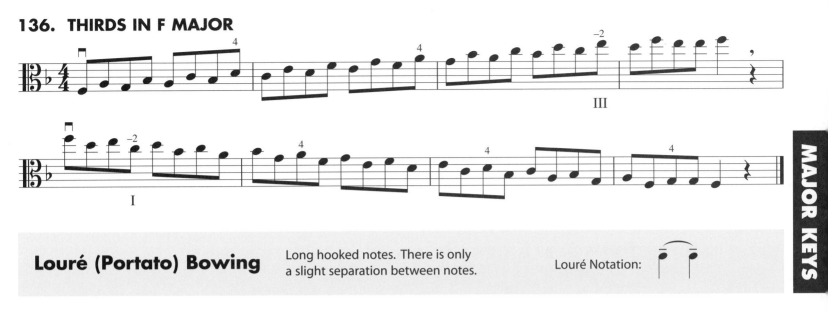

Louré (Portato) Bowing

Long hooked notes. There is only a slight separation between notes.

Louré Notation:

MAJOR KEYS

137. SIMPLE GIFTS

Shaker Melody

Moderato

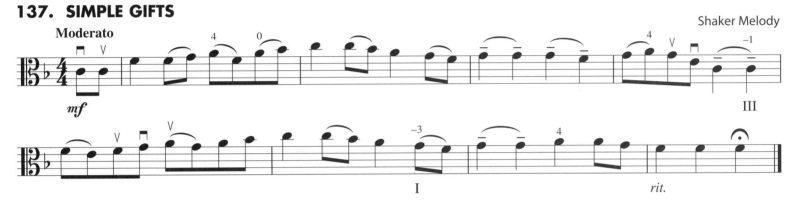

138. CHORALE IN F   A = Melody. B = Harmony.

J. S. Bach (1685–1750)

B♭ MAJOR

MAJOR KEYS

FINGER PATTERNS

Each finger pattern is a combination of whole steps and half steps. In the open hand pattern, a half step occurs between the open string and first finger. Other patterns have half steps between fingers 1–2, 2–3 or 3–4.

open hand   1–2   2–3   3–4

139. FINGER PATTERNS IN B♭ MAJOR – First Position

(violin, bass)

140. FINGER PATTERNS IN B♭ MAJOR – Third Position

(violin, bass)   III

141. B♭ MAJOR SCALE

142. B♭ MAJOR ARPEGGIO

143. THIRDS IN B♭ MAJOR

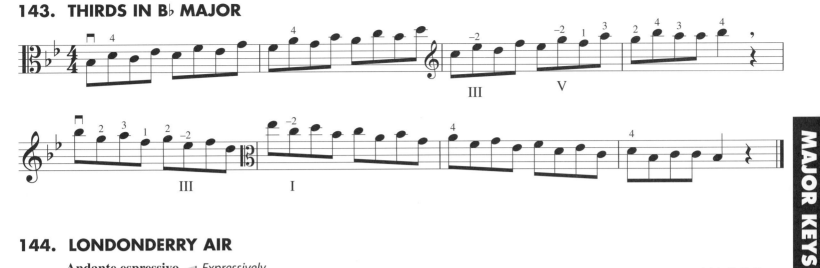

144. LONDONDERRY AIR

Andante espressivo ◁ *Expressively*

Irish Folk Song

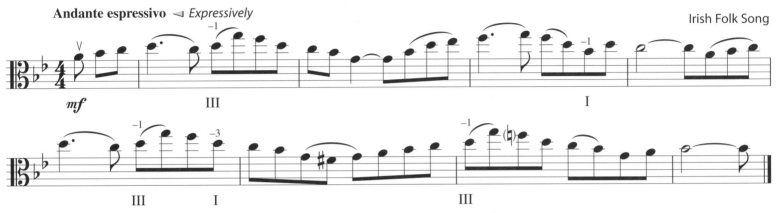

145. CHORALE IN B♭   A = Melody. B = Harmony.

J. S. Bach (1685–1750)

Eb MAJOR

FINGER PATTERNS

Each finger pattern is a combination of whole steps and half steps. In the open hand pattern, a half step occurs between the open string and first finger. Other patterns have half steps between fingers 1–2, 2–3 or 3–4.

open hand   1–2   2–3   3–4

146. FINGER PATTERNS IN Eb MAJOR – First Position

(violin, bass)

147. FINGER PATTERNS IN Eb MAJOR – Third Position

(violin, bass)   III

148. Eb MAJOR SCALE

149. Eb MAJOR ARPEGGIO

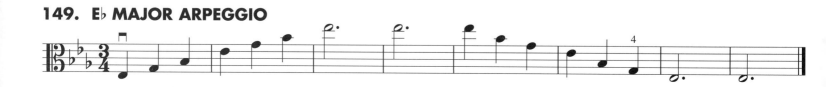

150. THIRDS IN E♭ MAJOR

MAJOR KEYS

HISTORY

German composer **Richard Wagner** was one of the leading opera writers in the mid to late 1800s. He brought musical drama to a new height with elaborate sets, large orchestras, and longer lengths of performance. His goal was to create a new art form where music and drama were of equal importance. During the same time, the first railroads were being built, the Americans fought a civil war, and Alexander Graham Bell invented the telephone.

151. PILGRIM'S CHORUS FROM TANNHÄUSER

Andante maestoso   Richard Wagner (1813–1883)

152. CHORALE IN E♭   A = Melody. B = Harmony.

J. S. Bach (1685–1750)

A MINOR

THEORY

Minor Keys

Minor keys and their scales sound different from major keys because of their different pattern of whole and half steps. Each minor key is *relative* or "related" to the major key with the same key signature.

The simplest form of a minor key is called **natural minor**. Two other types are **harmonic minor** and **melodic minor**, each of which have certain altered tones.

MINOR KEYS

153. A NATURAL MINOR

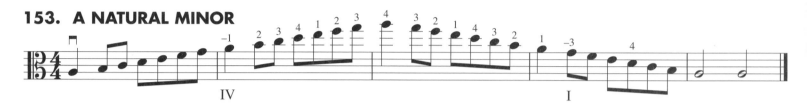

154. A HARMONIC MINOR

155. A MELODIC MINOR

156. A MINOR ARPEGGIO

157. SCARBOROUGH FAIR

158. GREENSLEEVES *Identify which form of the minor scale is used in this exercise.*

English Folk Tune

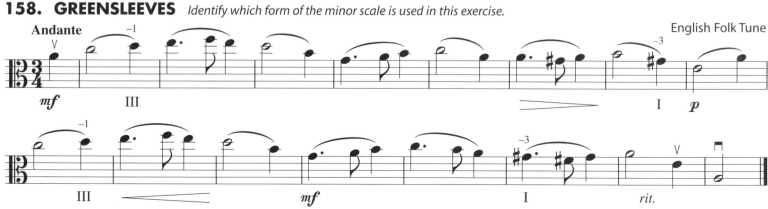

E MINOR

159. E NATURAL MINOR

160. E HARMONIC MINOR

161. E MELODIC MINOR

162. E MINOR ARPEGGIO

163. LA CINQUANTAINE

Gabriel Marie (1852–1882)

164. BOURÉE FROM SUITE IN E MINOR FOR LUTE

J.S. Bach (1685–1750)

MINOR KEYS

D MINOR

165. D NATURAL MINOR

166. D HARMONIC MINOR

167. D MELODIC MINOR

168. D MINOR ARPEGGIO

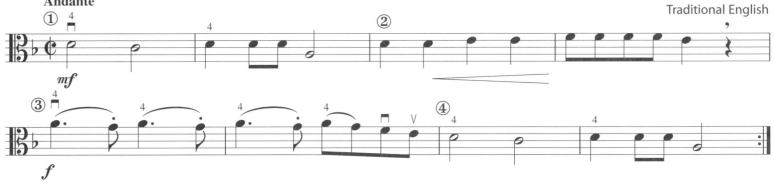

169. HEY, HO! NOBODY HOME – Round *Memorize this round. Then perform it for the class with a friend.*

Andante

Traditional English

Musical Form Musical form refers to how a piece of music is organized. One common form, ABA, is used in exercise 170. The first and third lines are the same (A) while the second line is different (B).

170. ZUM GALI GALI

Israeli Folk Tune

MINOR KEYS

34

G MINOR

171. G NATURAL MINOR

172. G HARMONIC MINOR

173. G MELODIC MINOR

174. G MINOR ARPEGGIO

HISTORY

Spirituals are religious folk songs originating within the African-American community. They were originally associated with work, recreation, or religious gatherings. Spirituals remain popular today, probably due to their strong rhythmic character and melodic lines.

175. JOSHUA

African-American Spiritual

Allegretto

176. PAT-A-PAN

French Carol

Moderato

MINOR KEYS

C MINOR

MINOR KEYS

177. C NATURAL MINOR

178. C HARMONIC MINOR

179. C MELODIC MINOR

180. C MINOR ARPEGGIO

HISTORY

Czech composer **Bedrich Smetana** was one of several 19th century composers who infused native folk themes into his compositions. "Moldau," named for a river in Bohemia, is one theme that is part of a collection of songs, entitled *Má Vlast* or " My Homeland." While composers of the 19th century were returning to their folk roots for inspiration, artists and writers were turning to more realistic reflections of current society. Charles Dickens was writing *David Copperfield* and *A Tale of Two Cities,* and Vincent van Gogh and Claude Monet both created images of urban and country life.

181. MOLDAU

Bedrich Smetana (1824–1884)

Allegretto

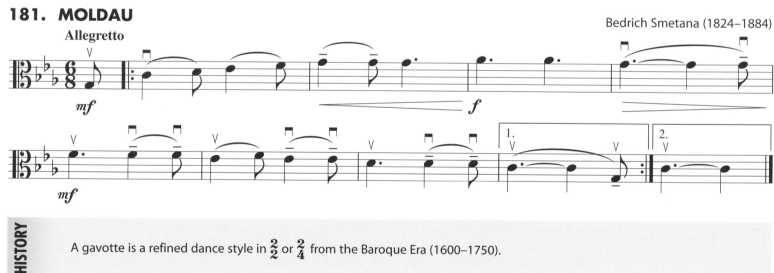

HISTORY

A gavotte is a refined dance style in $\frac{2}{2}$ or $\frac{2}{4}$ from the Baroque Era (1600–1750).

182. GAVOTTE

Andante

J.S. Bach (1685–1750)

Enharmonics

Enharmonics are two different note names which are both the same pitch *(see page 47 for more examples).*

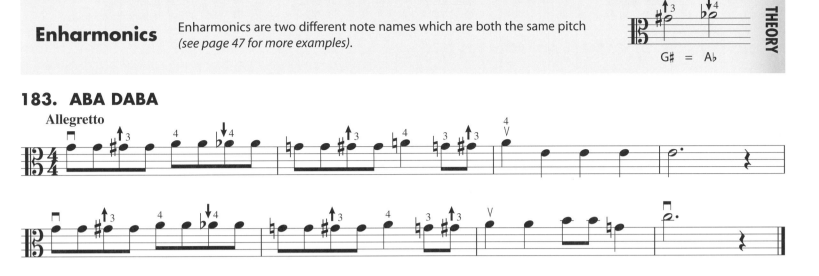

G♯ = A♭

THEORY

183. ABA DABA

Allegretto

CHROMATICS

A **Habañera** is a Cuban dance and song form in slow 2/4 meter. It is named after the city of Havana, the capital of Cuba. Made popular in the New World in the early 19th century, it was later carried over to Spain. In Spain, the rhythms of the Habañera were incorporated into many styles of Latin music. One of the most famous Habañeras is heard in Bizet's *Carmen*, written in 1875.

HISTORY

184. HABAÑERA

Georges Bizet (1838–1875)

Moderato

mp

Chromatic Scale

A chromatic scale is made up of consecutive half steps. It is usually written with sharps (♯) going up and flats (♭) going down.

THEORY

185. SHIFTING CHROMATIC FINGERING

186. CHROMATIC ETUDE

RHYTHM AND BOWING STUDIES

DOTTED RHYTHM STUDIES

NOTE DURATION CHART

1 e & a 2 e & a 3 e & a 4 e & a

187. *Write the counts below the notes before playing.*

188.

189.

190.

191.

192.

Sight-reading

Sight-reading means playing a musical piece for the first time. Review the word **S-T-A-R-S** to remind yourself what to look for before you play.

S — **Sharps or flats** in the key signature
T — **Time signature** and **tempo markings**
A — **Accidentals** not found in the key signature
R — **Rhythms**, silently counting the more difficult notes and rests
S — **Signs**, including dynamics, articulations, repeats and endings

Now sight-read the following exercise.

193.

RHYTHMS & BOWINGS

SIXTEENTH NOTE STUDIES

NOTE DURATION CHART

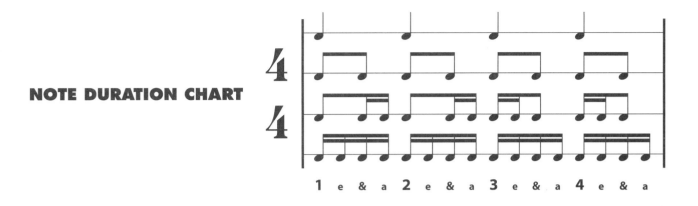

1 e & a 2 e & a 3 e & a 4 e & a

194. *Write the counts below the notes before playing.*

195.

196.

197.

198.

199.

Review **S-T-A-R-S** before sight-reading the following exercise.

200.

RHYTHMS & BOWINGS

SYNCOPATION STUDIES

NOTE DURATION CHART

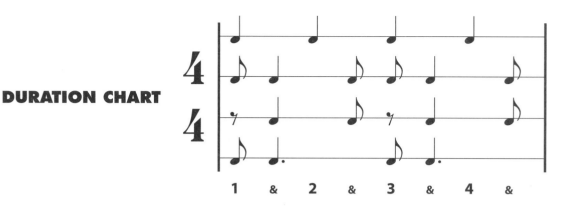

201. *Write the counts below the notes before playing.*

202.

203.

204.

205.

206.

Review **S-T-A-R-S** before sight-reading the following exercise.

207.

RHYTHMS & BOWINGS

6/8 RHYTHM STUDIES

NOTE DURATION CHART

1 + 2 + 3 + **4** + 5 + 6 +   **1** + 2 + 3 + **4** + 5 + 6 +

208. *Write the counts below the notes before playing.*

209.

210.

211.

212.

213.

RHYTHMS & BOWINGS

Review **S-T-A-R-S** before sight-reading the following exercise.

214.

VIBRATO WORKOUTS

You can add beauty and feeling to your sound with VIBRATO, a smooth pulsation of the tone. It is created by varying the pitch slightly. Use hand or arm vibrato as directed by your teacher. Once you have mastered this skill, add vibrato to your solo and ensemble playing.

HAND VIBRATO

ARM VIBRATO

1. At The Bout

Place your 3rd finger on top of the violin and your hand against the bout. Wave your hand or move your arm as directed by your teacher. In hand vibrato "at the bout," the wrist always touches the bout. For arm vibrato, the wrist remains straight as it moves away. For both, flex the first knuckle.

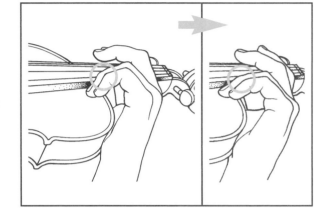

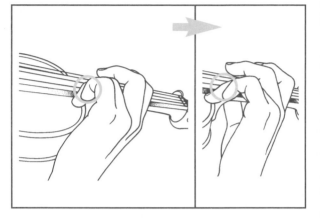

2. On The String

Now do the same motion with your 3rd finger on the A string.

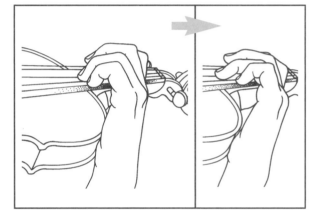

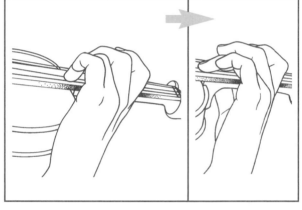

3. Lend A Helping Hand

Touch the bout with 2 fingers of your right hand as shown. This begins to separate your left hand from the bout.

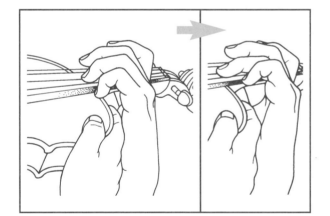

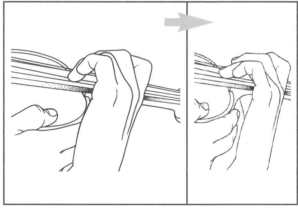

4. Back Down The String

Place your left hand in a lower position with your right hand fingers touching the arm just below the wrist. When you start to feel comfortable with the motion, remove your right hand.

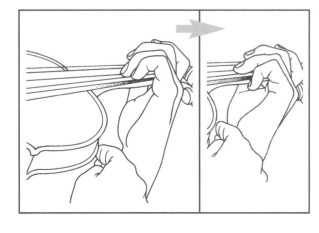

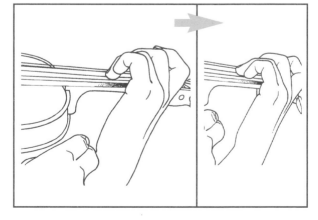

 Master these Workouts before using VIBRATO in your playing!

VIBRATO

THIRD AND FIRST POSITION VIBRATO EXERCISES

First practice these vibrato exercises without bowing. The lower part of the vibrato motion is shown in small notes, which do not denote actual pitches. You may proceed with the bow once your teacher has approved your left hand motion.

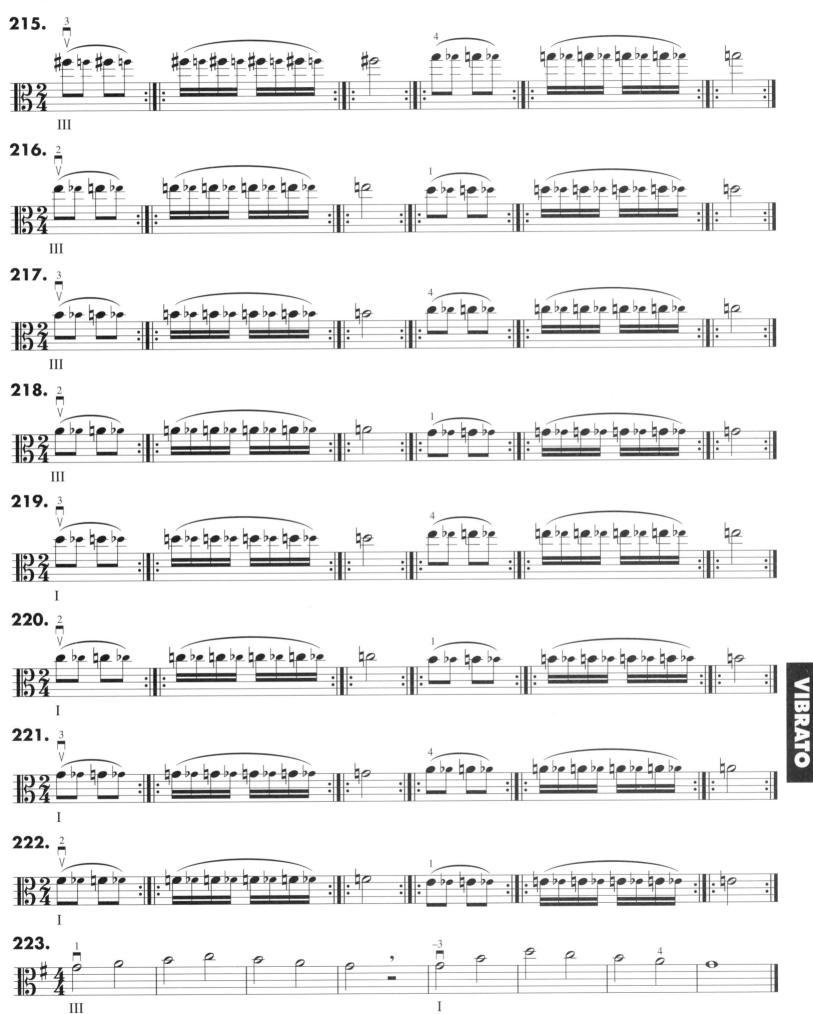

Spiccato Bowing

A light bouncing stroke in the lower half of the bow. Play spiccato (off the string) or staccato (on the string) as directed by your teacher. Spiccato is normally used in medium and faster tempos.

Spiccato Notation:

224.

225.

226.

227.

228. SLAVIC FOLK SONG

Allegretto

229.

230. CAN CAN

Presto

Jacques Offenbach (1819–1880)

SPICCATO

FOR VIOLAS ONLY

FOURTH POSITION ON THE D AND A STRINGS

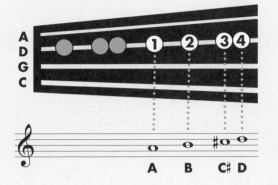
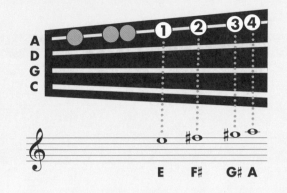

A.

B.

FIFTH POSITION ON THE D AND A STRINGS

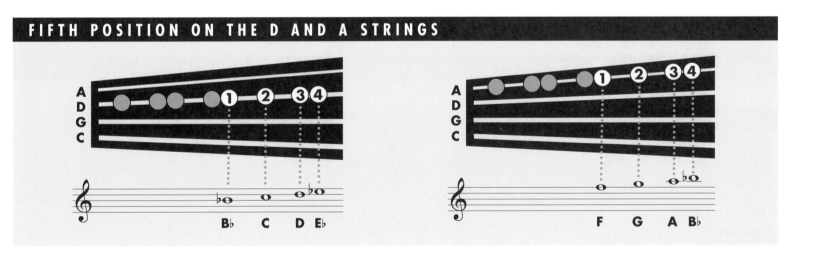

C.

D.

VIOLA FINGERING CHART

Finger Patterns These fingering charts include all half steps in the positions shown. Use a combination of half steps and whole steps for most finger patterns.

FIRST AND THIRD POSITION

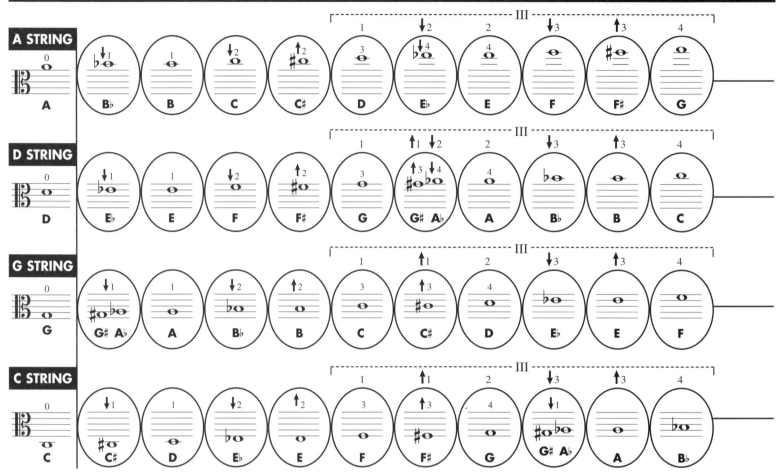

SECOND POSITION

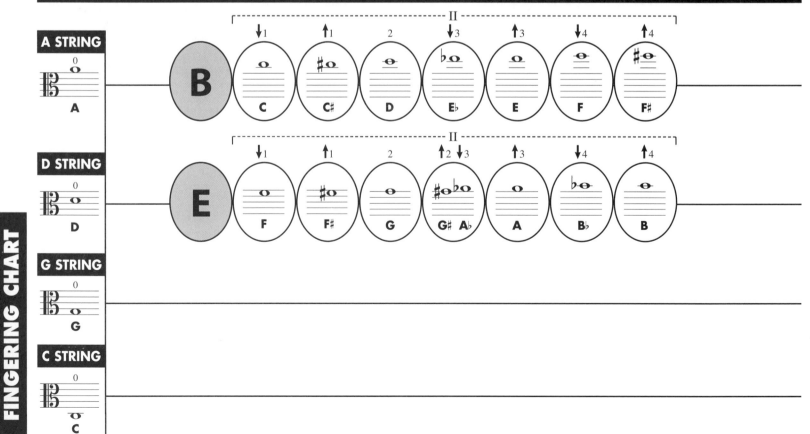

FOR VIOLAS ONLY

FOURTH POSITION ON THE D AND A STRINGS

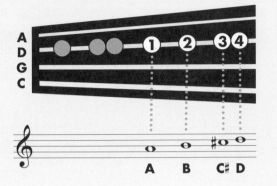

A B C# D

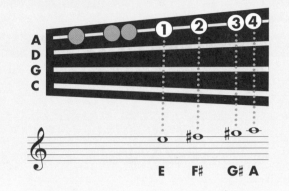

E F# G# A

A.

B.

FIFTH POSITION ON THE D AND A STRINGS

Bb C D Eb

F G A Bb

C.

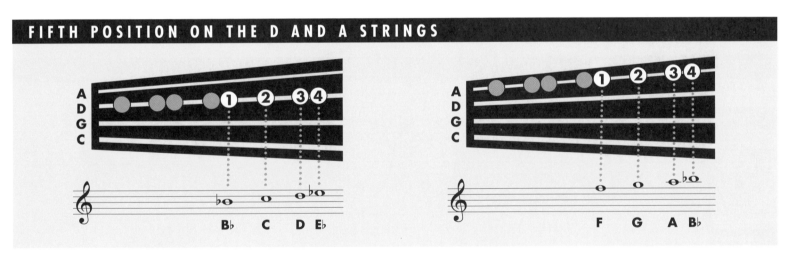

D.

VIOLA FINGERING CHART

Finger Patterns

These fingering charts include all half steps in the positions shown. Use a combination of half steps and whole steps for most finger patterns.

FIRST AND THIRD POSITION

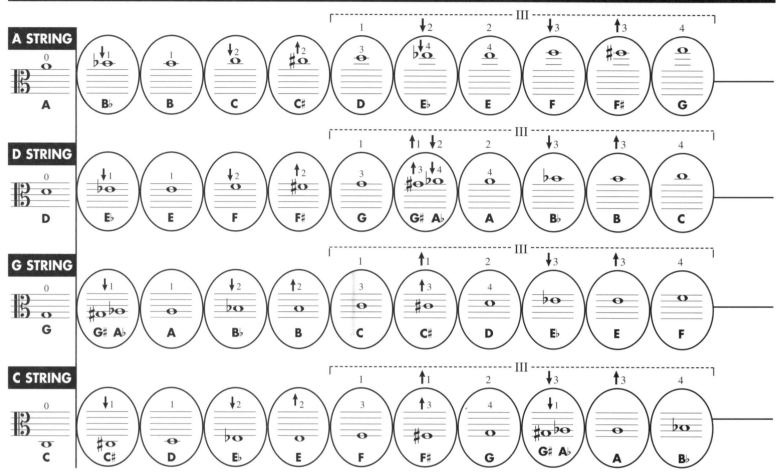

SECOND POSITION

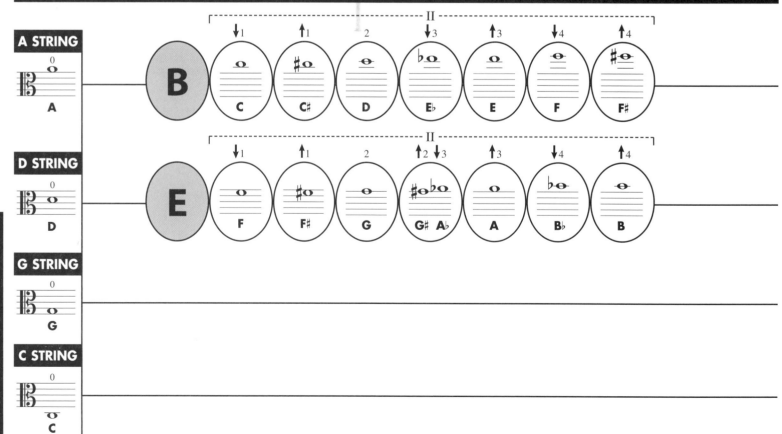

VIOLA FINGERING CHART

FOURTH POSITION

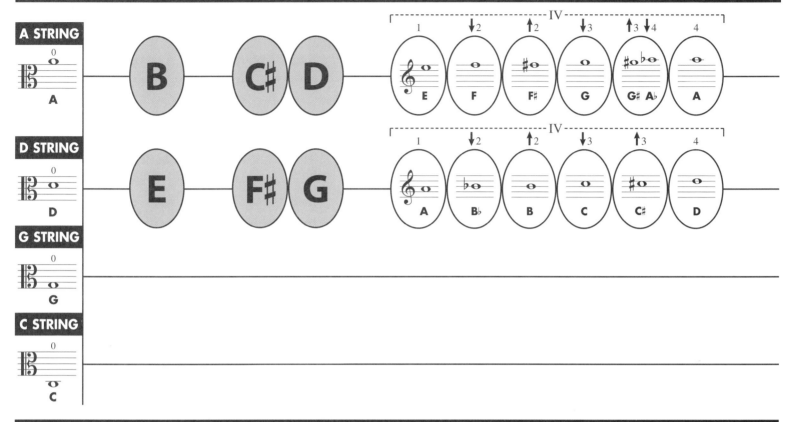

FIFTH POSITION

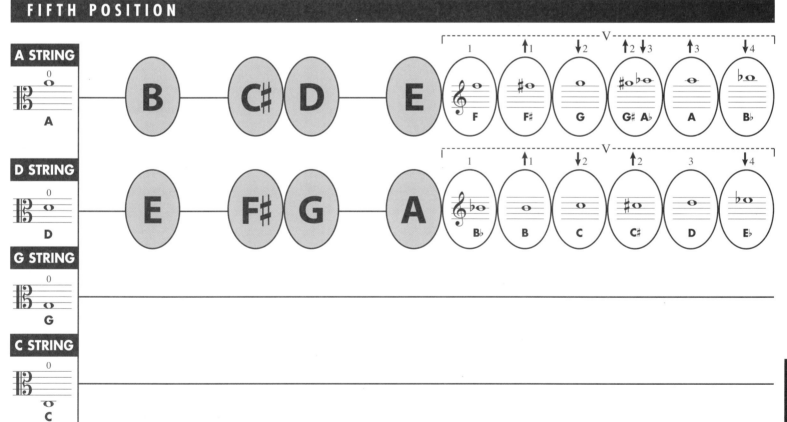

Enharmonics

All sharps and flats have enharmonics which are usually played at the same place on the string by the next finger up or down. For example, an A♭ on the D string in 1st position is played by low 4th finger at the same spot where G♯ can be played by high 3rd finger. Common enharmonics:

COMPOSITION

Composition

Composition is the art of writing original music. A composer often begins by creating a melody made up of individual **phrases**, like short musical "sentences." Some melodies have phrases that seem to answer or respond to "question" phrases.

Q. AND A. *Write your own "answer" to the following melodies.*

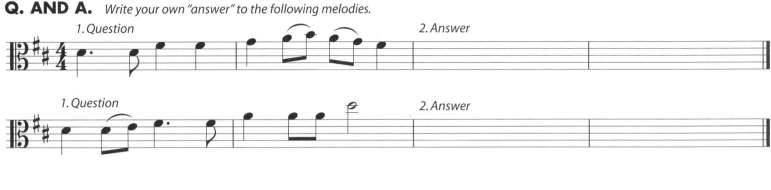

YOU NAME IT: _____ *Now write your own music.*

 **REFERENCE INDEX**

Definitions (pg.)

Composers

World Music